The adventures of Pinkie

The Adventures of Pinkie is a book that will inform children and adults on incurable muscle diseases in a light and child-friendly way. Parents and family members can use the book to start a talk with their children. The animals in the story appeal to the imagination and the children will be able to identify themselves with them. Central is the importance of friendship and the creation of memories.

www.aerialmediacom.nl
www.facebook.com/Aerialmediacompany

ISBN 978-94-026-00149-7

Cover design: Joost van Pinxten
Typesetting: Teo van Gerwen Design
Translation: Marion Singor
Editing: Jude Irwin, Word Doctor

Aerial Media Company bv.
Postbus 6088
4000 HB Tiel, The Netherlands

The adventures of Pinkie

ANTON MINKELS

AERIAL MEDIA COMPANY

It was a beautiful day. The sun was shining high in the sky and there was not a cloud in sight. But things were not going to go well on this sunny day...

Pinkie was playing in the farmyard with his brothers and sisters. His friends Sam and Ollie were there too, of course. Their favourite game was tag. They were a crazy bunch, screaming, laughing and chasing each other. As always, Pinkie's eldest brother Johnny just couldn't be tagged – though they all gave it their best shot. There was no denying it – he was just the fastest sheep in the whole flock.

Pinkie had noticed something in the last few days though. Johnny had tripped a couple of times. Just like that, for no reason. Today it happened again. Johnny was running so fast – you could see he was thinking he had eight legs instead of four – and the whole gang was after him as usual. Suddenly, he made a sharp turn to the right. But his hind legs slid away, as if they still wanted to run straight on. He rolled over and over, right through a great big puddle.

"Yeah, I've tagged you!" laughed Pinkie, tapping Johnny with his leg. Even Farmer Tom, who was just passing, could not hide a smile.

Johnny gazed around, looking dazed. His beautiful white curls were covered in mud and he was black from head to hoof. The others all laughed their heads off.

"Tats not bunny!" yelled Johnny, rather angrily.

"What?" replied Ollie. He did not understand a word Johnny had said.

"Tats not bunny!" cried Johnny again, even angrier this time. The others were laughing even louder now.

"But what does he mean?" spluttered Kevin. Kevin was the youngest sheep in the flock. He himself often had trouble talking. All the other sheep were now rolling on the floor hysterically.

Poor Johnny! First he had rolled through the mud so spectacularly and now he was talking really strangely. Some of the other sheep were complaining that their tummies were sore from laughing.

But Johnny wasn't laughing. A big tear rolled slowly down his cheek. Nobody noticed when he got up and walked to the stable, feeling sad.

That afternoon the farm smelled delicious. The farmer's wife Mollie

had baked apple pies, and nobody on earth could bake apple pies

like hers. Sadly, Pinkie knew the pies were not for him or the rest

of the flock. There were some people coming to visit, and they

would get the pies – lucky things!

Pinkie was tired of playing, but the delicious smell was stopping

him from going to sleep.

"Hmmm, what if I just…?" thought Pinkie. He looked at Ollie. He

knew he would be up for an adventure.

"Pssst Ollie, wake up," whispered Pinkie.

"Huh?" murmured Ollie sleepily.

"Apple pie!" hissed Pinkie. Pinkie didn't have to say it twice - Ollie

immediately knew what he was talking about. He jumped to

attention, laughing and nodding enthusiastically.

"Shall we ask Sam too?" asked Ollie.

"No, just leave him," said Ollie. "He'd probably be too scared or say it is too cold for him. Come on, let's go!"

Off they ran. They could already taste the delicious pies in their imagination. Outside the stable, they saw Johnny, who was still looking very sad.

"Johnny, are you coming with us?" said Pinkie. "We're off to eat some apple pie!" Johnny's face immediately broke into a smile.

"Yummy!" he shouted. "I'm in!"

As they nosed their way into the kitchen, Pinkie asked Johnny if he was still angry. "Oh no, not anymore," replied Johnny.

"You were talking in such a funny way though," ventured Pinkie.

"I wasn't doing it on purpose," explained Johnny. "I was just trying to say I didn't like it."

"Oh?" mused Pinkie.

"Yessss!" shouted Ollie suddenly. "THREE pies! AND there's no one here! Come on – grab one each!" He scampered into the kitchen, where indeed three shiny apple pies were waiting on the table. The aroma coming from the pies was heavenly.

As if they had not had anything to eat in weeks, the three sheep fell ravenously upon the pies. They tasted truly scrumptious! In no time, there were three empty plates and three very satisfied guzzlers on the table. But just as they were climbing down from the table, Mollie came into the kitchen.

"Hey, what's going on?" she cried. Quick as a flash, Pinkie, Ollie and Johnny dived through Mollie's legs and headed for the kitchen door. Once they got outside they ran as if their lives depended on it.

"Well, of all the double-crossing double-knitted balls of wool!" shouted Mollie, giving chase.

"Faster," cried Johnny. Pinkie and Ollie were already running for all they were worth, and Johnny was out in front as always. But Mollie was getting closer…and closer…and closer to Pinkie and Ollie. When Johnny got to the end of the farm, he took the corner at full speed. But, his back legs slipped out from under him and he slid along the ground once again.

"What are you doing?" screamed Ollie who was the first to pass Johnny. But Pinkie stopped running. He walked slowly towards his brother. But Johnny did not move. Mollie was right behind Pinkie. She did not look angry any more. She wasn't laughing either. She looked strange.

"Tom," she cried in a frightened voice. Her husband was in the garden. "Come quickly, we need to take Johnny to the doctor, now!"

The flock waited anxiously for the farmer and his wife to bring Johnny back to the farm – it seemed to take forever. When they finally arrived home, their faces were sad. Mollie looked like she had been crying.

"Why are you so sad?" asked Pinkie, feeling a little scared.

"Johnny is ill," said Mollie. "Very ill. It's something to do with his muscles. He won't get better. In a while he won't be able to walk, eat or talk any more".

"Of course he will," said Pinkie. "There must be pills or injections or something? Or they could operate on him? Or...?" Mollie looked at Pinkie with tears in her eyes. She shook her head.

"I'm sorry, Pinkie," sobbed Mollie.

"No, it can't be true!" shouted Pinkie. "Johnny is the fastest sheep of all of us. He'll be able to run again soon, of course he will! I don't believe it!" Mollie put her arms around Johnny and Pinkie. She said nothing. She was crying.

Sadly, Mollie was right. As the year went on, Johnny had more and

more trouble walking. Running was out of the question altogether.

Even a short walk from the stable to the yard was too tiring. Tom and

Mollie came to the stable several times a day to feed Johnny. Soon

he could no longer chew and swallow properly, because his muscles

had become too weak. When he tried to talk he was more and more

difficult to understand. Everyone felt terribly ashamed about the

time they had laughed at him. But Johnny did not mind. After all, they

didn't know he was sick.

They did not play much outside that year. All the sheep wanted to stay close to Johnny. They helped him to drink and made sure he was lying comfortably in the hay. The sheep were often very sad. They wanted to help Johnny, but there wasn't much they could do. Fortunately, Johnny stayed cheerful and liked joking with his friends and talking about the wonderful adventures they'd had together.

"Where does Johnny actually go to when he does not wake up anymore?" asked Sam one day. All the animals were startled by the question.

"I have heard that when a sheep goes to sleep forever he becomes a cloud," said Pinkie. "Then he finds a nice spot in the sky and goes there."

"A cloud?" replied Ollie thoughtfully. "Those big white things in the sky?" Pinkie nodded.

"Wow! Then a cloud will look just like you Johnny!" smiled Sam.

Johnny had to laugh. "And I'll always be able to watch over you from up there."

All too soon, the day came when Johnny could not go on any more. He found it harder and harder to breathe. He was so tired that all he wanted to do was to sleep.

"We are going to take Johnny to the doctor," sobbed Mollie. "He really needs to rest."

"Will he come back when he's had his rest?" asked little Kevin, who was struggling to understand what was happening. Mollie smiled at him.

"No Kevin, Johnny is not coming back. He is so tired that he will not wake up again." Kevin cried very big tears. "Tats not bunny!" he sniffed. Everyone stared at Kevin.

"Ohhh," he stammered. "I didn't mean to say that!" A soft chuckle came from the hay. Johnny was smiling at Kevin, and he gave him a little wink. Then Farmer Tom lifted Johnny up. Johnny gazed around the stable one last time and looked at each of his friends in turn. He smiled and closed his eyes.

Tom and Mollie came home at the end of the day. They walked slowly to the stable, where all the sheep were sitting together, feeling sad.

"I've got something for you," said Mollie, and took a huge frame out of the bag she was carrying. There was a beautiful picture in the frame, of Pinkie, Ollie and Johnny. They were standing on a kitchen table, each eating an apple pie…

"I had such a laugh that day," explained Mollie. "Before I yelled at you, I took this picture. You didn't even notice because you were too busy gobbling down pies!"

A smile spread across her face. "This picture will take pride of place in the stable. Then you can always see Johnny like this. Not as the sheep with a muscle disease, but as the fastest sheep in the herd. The sheep that had so many wonderful adventures with all of you."

"Cool!" screamed Pinkie enthusiastically. "We have this picture, the cloud and all our memories. Johnny will stay with us forever!"

About MND/ALS

Motor neurone disease (MND) is a progressive disease that attacks the motor neurones, or nerves, in the brain and spinal cord. This means messages gradually stop reaching muscles, which leads to weakness and wasting.

MND can affect how you walk, talk, eat, drink and breathe. However, not all symptoms necessarily happen to everyone and it is unlikely they will all develop at the same time, or in any specific order. Although there is currently no cure for MND, symptoms can be managed to help you achieve the best possible quality of life.

For more information:

United Kingdom:
The Motor Neurone Disease Association is the only national charity in England, Wales and Northern Ireland focused on MND care, research and campaigning:
www.mndassociation.org

United States of America:
Established in 1985, **The ALS Association** is the only national non-profit organization fighting Lou Gehrig's Disease on every front: www.alsa.org

For more international information please contact:
The International Alliance of ALS/MND Associations: www.alsmndalliance.org